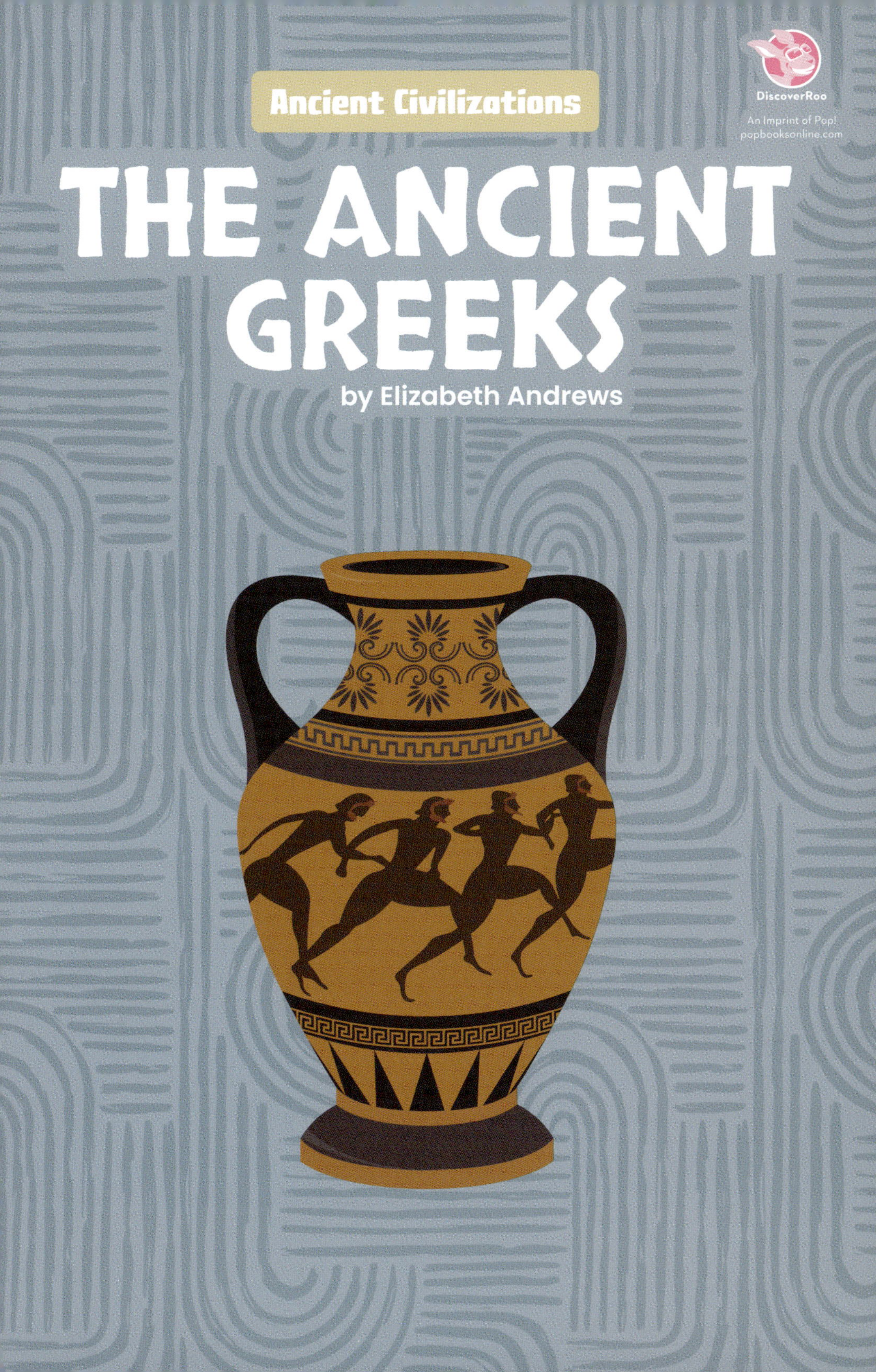

THE ANCIENT GREEKS

by Elizabeth Andrews

WELCOME TO DiscoverRoo!

This book is filled with videos, puzzles, games, and more! Scan the QR codes* while you read, or visit the website below to make this book pop.

popbooksonline.com/anc-greeks

abdobooks.com

Published by Pop!, a division of ABDO, PO Box 398166, Minneapolis, Minnesota 55439. Copyright © 2023 by Abdo Consulting Group, Inc. International copyrights reserved in all countries. No part of this book may be reproduced in any form without written permission from the publisher. DiscoverRoo™ is a trademark and logo of Pop!.

Printed in the United States of America, North Mankato, Minnesota.

102022
012023

THIS BOOK CONTAINS RECYCLED MATERIALS

Cover Photo: Getty Images, Shutterstock Images
Interior Photos: Shutterstock Images, Getty Images, Gianni Dagli Orti/Shutterstock
Editor: Emily Dreher
Series Designer: Laura Graphenteen

Library of Congress Control Number: 2022941117

Publisher's Cataloging-in-Publication Data
Names: Andrews, Elizabeth, author.
Title: The ancient Greeks / by Elizabeth Andrews
Description: Minneapolis, Minnesota : Pop!, 2023 | Series: Ancient civilizations | Includes online resources and index.
Identifiers: ISBN 9781098243258 (lib. bdg.) | ISBN 9781098243951 (ebook)
Subjects: LCSH: Greece--History--Juvenile literature. | Greeks--Juvenile literature. | Ancient civilization--Juvenile literature. | Indigenous peoples--Social life and customs--Juvenile literature. | Cultural anthropology--Juvenile literature.
Classification: DDC 972.01--dc23

*Scanning QR codes requires a web-enabled smart device with a QR code reader app and a camera.

TABLE OF CONTENTS

CHAPTER 1
Great Greek Beginning 4

CHAPTER 2
The Greek People 10

CHAPTER 3
Greek Mythology 16

CHAPTER 4
Ancient Thinkers 22

Making Connections 30

Glossary 31

Index 32

Online Resources 32

GREAT GREEK BEGINNING

Nearly 5,000 years ago, the ancient Greek civilization began on the beautiful, rocky land along the sparkling Mediterranean Sea. Ancient Greece spread from present-day Greece to the Middle East and northern Africa. The first civilization

recorded in Greece was the Minoans, who

existed until 1500 BCE. They were followed

by the Mycenaeans, who lasted through

1100 BCE.

Life in ancient Greece was simple and steady until 700 BCE. Around 650 BCE, the Greeks started spreading out.

Greek regions were divided into **city-states**. Each one was a part of Greece but operated independently. City-states lacked physical borders. Instead, they were defined by the people who counted themselves as citizens.

City-states were separate from each other, but the lifestyles of each place were alike. Greece's rocky and mountainous land made communication difficult among city-states. Communities rarely mixed. In fact, the city-states were known to pick fights with each other.

City-states were led by tyrants. A single man would take control of the land. His family would rule for a few **generations**. Eventually, another man would fight for control. The power would change hands.

Outside forces tried to take over Greece. Persia sat to the east. It had a better army than the

Greeks. But Persia's army faced strong and **passionate** Greek soldiers. They were proud to defend their homeland. After many battles, the Greeks officially defeated the Persians in 479 BCE. Athens was the most powerful city-state in Greece at that time.

CHAPTER 2

THE GREEK PEOPLE

Daily life for ancient Greeks was similar from state to state. However, it was different between the rich and poor and the men and women. Most Greeks were farmers and traders. Farmers focused on

trying to survive. Greek land was difficult

to farm, but easy access to water made

it possible.

Almost every citizen in Greece owned slaves. The enslaved people were usually outsiders from warring **city-states**. They lived hard lives working in **mines** and tending fields. However, some were treated as members of the family.

Women in ancient Greece had very few rights. They stayed home to care for their property, their slaves, and most family matters. They were not supposed to be seen in public. Lower-class women left the home to get water and do outdoor chores. They didn't have slaves to do the work. However, poor women still could not interact with the public.

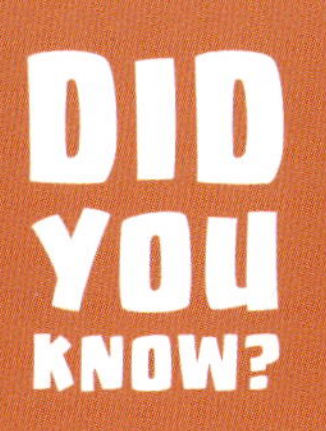

Women took care of loved ones' graves. They brought **offerings** and decorated the sites.

Men in ancient Greece had the most rights and freedoms. Wealthy men kept many enslaved people who cared for their land. Their wives managed the homes, so men had free time for intellectual and athletic activities. Physical fitness was important in ancient Greece because people often had to defend their homes.

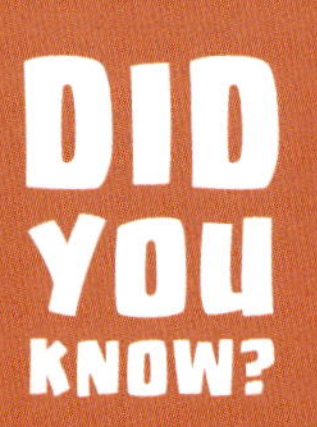

DID YOU KNOW? Wealthy boys got the most education. They learned about math, reading and writing, and music.

Men and women wore tunic-style squares of cloth. Tunics were wool or linen depending on the season. They were styled with pins and belts. Greeks ate mostly bread, fruits, vegetables, fish, and cheese. They would get other proteins from eggs, and milk from sheep and goats. Meat was usually only enjoyed at religious festivals.

Ancient Greeks believed in many gods.

They were famous for their mythology.

They believed the gods lived on top of

Mount Olympus in northern Greece.

Humans were not allowed to climb up

the mountain.

Each Greek god had certain powers and weaknesses. They oversaw specific places and things, like homes and farming. The gods and goddesses looked like humans.

A giant statue of Athena once stood in the Parthenon of Athens. It was a temple where people could go to honor her.

Zeus was the king of gods. He ruled the skies. His brother Poseidon ruled the sea. Their other brother, Hades, ruled the underworld and the dead. Zeus had many children. Athena was his favorite. She was the goddess of wisdom and war. Ares was Zeus's least favorite child. He was the god of warfare.

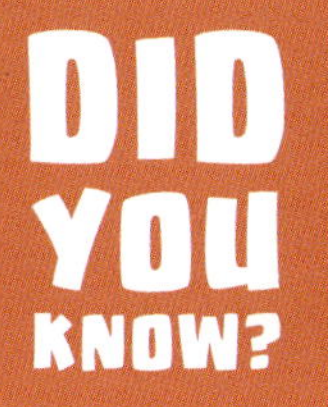

DID YOU KNOW?

Athena was the patron goddess of Athens. The city was dedicated to her.

Ancient Greeks used the myths about gods and goddesses to explain natural happenings. The myth about Persephone, goddess of spring, explains the seasons. When Persephone is in the underworld with her husband Hades, the weather is cold and dark. Plants die. When she returns to Earth for half the year, the sun shines and plants bloom.

Greek festivals and ceremonies marked changing seasons and special days. Dionysia is a festival in March. It honored the god of wine and celebrations, Dionysus. At this festival, play writers competed to give the best performance. The Olympic games honored Zeus. Men competed in chariot races, physical fights, and throwing matches. These two festivals changed over time, but they are still held today.

The first documented Olympic Games took place in 776 BCE.

ANCIENT THINKERS

The ancient Greeks took big steps in politics and **philosophy**. In 507 BCE, a leader in the **city-state** of Athens introduced the first known democracy. Democracy means "rule by the people." Life for the poor was much harder than

it was for rich people. Some government

leaders wanted to change that and make

life better for all Greeks.

Athens' democracy inspired some governments that exist today.

Democracy was a new system of creating laws and choosing leaders. All male citizens in Athens could vote at meetings held 40 times a year. They voted about city officials, war, and how the city's money would be spent. Women, slaves, and people who weren't from Athens could not vote. Every decision was made based on who or what earned the most votes. In the past, only one person had that kind of power. Courts full of **jurors** held people accountable for following laws.

A symposium was an event in Athens where free men gathered. They tested new ways of thinking. Philosophers, like Socrates, Plato, and Aristotle, were popular. They gave speeches about ways Greek culture had succeeded and failed. They also spoke about ways Greece could change for the better. Math and science were also studied and discussed at a symposium.

Men would eat, drink, and watch entertainment at a symposium.

Outside Athens, city-states were still ruled by individuals. In 336 BCE, Alexander the Great changed everything. Alexander grouped all city-states under his rule. He was a powerful war general who **conquered** land beyond Greece. He spread Greek culture everywhere his army went. Ancient Greece's control spread south all the way to Egypt, and east all the way to Asia.

Eventually his army tired out and turned back once it reached India. Alexander's constant wars weakened

Greece. The civilization fell to the Romans in 146 BCE. However, ancient Greece left its mark on the world in ways that can still be seen today.

ANCIENT GREEK EMPIRE (323 BCE)

KEY — **Alexander the Great's peak Greek empire**

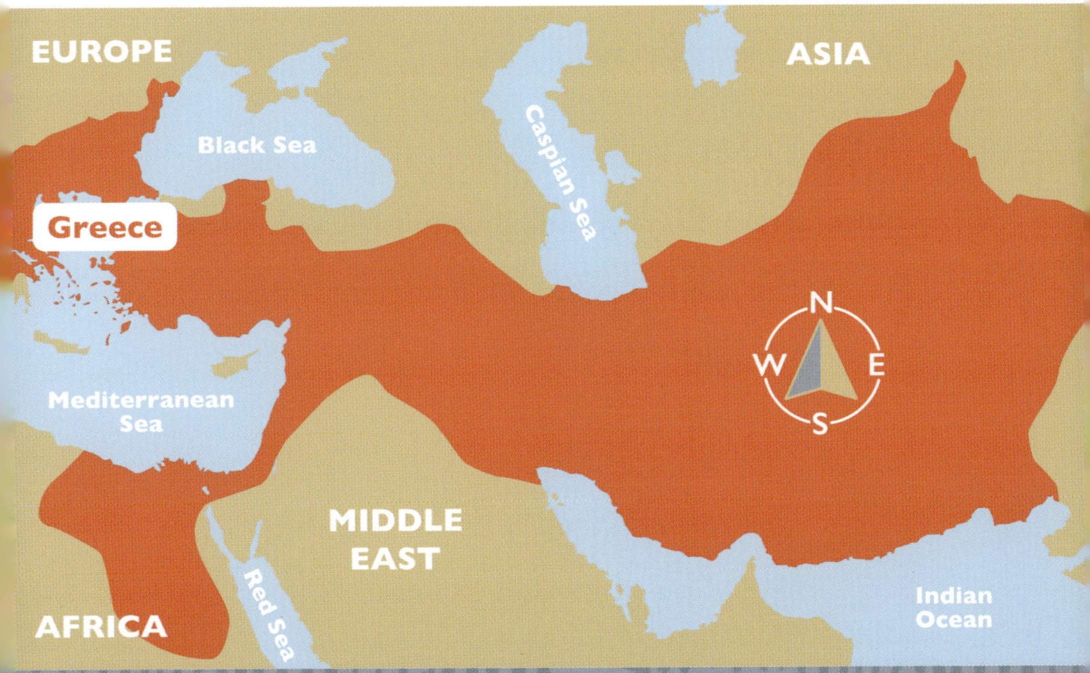

MAKING CONNECTIONS

TEXT-TO-SELF

What Greek god or goddess are you most interested in learning more about? Why?

TEXT-TO-TEXT

Have you read any other books about ancient civilizations? What did they have in common with ancient Greece?

TEXT-TO-WORLD

What did ancient Greece give to the world? How might the world be different if ancient Greece hadn't existed?

GLOSSARY

city-state — a state made of a city and its surrounding territory.

conquer — to gain land by force.

generation — the period of time between the birth of parents and the birth of their children.

juror — someone called to a court of law who decides the outcome of a case.

mine — a deep hole or area of holes made in the earth. The Greeks mined materials such as copper, iron, and silver.

offering — a gift given as a form of worship.

passionate — capable of or expressing strong feeling.

philosophy — the study of the meaning of life, truth, knowledge, and other important human ideas.

INDEX

Alexander the Great, 28–29

Athens, 9, 19, 22, 25–26

city-states, 7–9, 12, 22, 28

democracy, 22, 25

festival, 20–21

fighting, 8–9, 28–29

gods and goddesses, 16–17, 19–21

men, 8, 10, 14–15, 25–26

Mount Olympus, 16

slaves, 12–14, 25

Sparta, 8

symposium, 26

women, 8, 10, 13, 15, 25

popbooksonline.com/anc-greeks

*Scanning QR codes requires a web-enabled smart device with a QR code reader app and a camera.